"Help! There's a Toddler in My House!"

Fun, Easy Activities for Every Room of Your Home

Nancy Kelly

Robins Lane Press

a division of Gryphon House, Inc.

www.robinslane.com

LIVING ROOM

KITCHEN

DINING ROOM

NURSERY

BATHROOM

Library of Congress Cataloging-in-Publication Data

Kelly, Nancy, 1957–
    Help! There's a toddler in my house : easy, fun activities
for every room of your home /
Nancy Kelly.
        p.   cm.
    Includes index
    ISBN 158904-000-7
    1. Play. 2. Creative activities and seat work. 3. Toddlers.
    I. Title.
HQ782.K35   2001
0649'.5—dc21   2001023714

Cover and interior design by Bartko Design
Cover photography by Sharon Hoogstraten
Interior illustrations by Shauna Mooney Kawasaki

Published by Robins Lane Press
A division of Gryphon House
10726 Tucker St., Beltsville, MD 20705 U.S.A.
Copyright © 2001 by Nancy Kelly
Printed in the United States of America
International Standard Book Number: 158904-000-7
01 02 03 04 05 06   15 14 13 12 11 10 9 8 7 6 5 4 3 2 1

CONTENTS

ACKNOWLEDGMENTS

THREE YEARS AGO, I needed safe and fun

activities for my son, and could find no resources specific to toddlers. This book began with that challenge and grew as I accumulated ideas through research, as well as my own (and Teddy's) invention. The ideas it contains have been field-tested both at home, with my child, and in the classes I began teaching for toddlers and their mothers.

My acknowledgments start with all the moms and their children who participated in those early classes, as well as the subsequent ones at Toddler Place. I also want to thank my dear Cheri Hoffman for helping make Toddler Place possible—not to mention her numerous and daily acts of friendship and support. Finally, for making the book a reality, my gratitude to Justin Rood, tireless editor and publisher, who shaped potential into product, made "good" into "better," and kept all the balls in the air with humor and savvy.

Expanding beyond Maryland, I give thanks to Jen Hontz for her sisterly love and care, enthusiasm and validation. And to my mentor, Dr. Lil Russo, many thanks for the countless hours she's given as confidante, critic, cheerleader and coach.

Full circle, my acknowledgments return to my family: Ed, my best supporter and friend.

And, of course, Teddy, who started it all.

The GROUND RULES

1. Everything you use with your toddler should be either edible or at least nontoxic. The average 18-month-old is still putting many (or all) things into his mouth.

2. Fun is in the process, not the finished masterpiece.

3. Don't expect your child to finish every project.

4. Don't worry about buying specialty products. Make do with what you have, or do without. I promise they won't know the difference.

5. A lot of these activities can be messy, so before you begin cover the floor with an old shower curtain or some newspaper. Cover the table as well: Plastic tablecloths, butcher paper and/or waxed paper work well for most activities.

LIVING ROOM

KITCHEN

DINING ROOM

NURSERY

BATHROOM

6. Keep your child in a bib at minimum. (My son wears the same "painter" shirt when we do any activity involving food coloring, chocolate or anything else that can stain.)

7. Craft activities are not "busy work" for toddlers. You cannot leave your child alone with the applesauce fingerpaint and take a shower!

8. Remember basic toddler food safety (avoid nuts, popcorn, hard candy and raw eggs) as well as your child's own allergies (milk, food coloring, peanut butter).

9. Nothing will hold your child's interest for very long. So don't plan to make, say, enough holiday cookies for your six brothers and sisters and their families. Consider a half-dozen edible cookies an unequivocal victory.

10. Do an activity only as long as your child finds it fun and interesting.

"Help!
There's a Toddler *in* My House!"

CHAPTER 1

In the LIVING ROOM

Clear some space! These games are for the loud and noisy part of the day and should provide an outlet for that endless toddler energy.

Pillow Play

Materials
Pillows

These are great ways for even the youngest toddler to exercise gross motor skills.

- Pile up throw pillows and sofa cushions on the floor for your child to climb on and roll over.
- Hide underneath a pile of pillows and sing "Pop Goes the Weasel." On "Pop," jump out from underneath the pile.
- Build a nest out of the cushions and pretend to be birds.
- Build a cave and pretend you are bears.
- Make tunnels and pretend you are trains.

Singing "I've Been Working on the Railroad" and "She'll be Comin' 'Round the Mountain" adds to this activity

- Build a house from the large cushions and play "The Three Little Pigs."

Be careful with these games, as toddler exuberance can sometimes lead to slips and falls.

Obstacle Course

Materials
Pillows
Small stool
Shoebox
Textured materials
* such as a blanket,*
* cotton balls or egg cartons*
Box (optional)

Pillows also make great toddler obstacle courses.

Spread the pillows and cushions around on the floor. Add a small stool to climb up on, a shoebox to jump over, textured material such as egg cartons, a blanket or cotton balls to walk on and a large box or laundry basket to crawl through or sit in. Let your toddler explore the course.

 Styrofoam egg cartons make a better sound than cardboard ones, but if your child puts everything in her mouth, stick with the cardboard ones. For the same reason, you may want to substitute large scraps of material for the cotton balls.

Variation
Make the obstacle course a jungle: climb the mountain (stool), jump the stream (shoebox), wade through the quicksand (cotton balls) and crawl through the tunnel (box).

 Make sure the box is open at both ends. (Some toddlers do not like entering a box closed at one end.)

Crocodile in the Water

Materials

Pillows

Crocodile puppet (optional)

For this game, spread the pillows on the floor. Make chomping motions with the puppet and shout, "Crocodile in the water!" Help your toddler get to the safety of dry land (a pillow). Play again, this time chomping and shouting, "Croc on the land." Now help him escape back to the water (floor).

The puppet isn't absolutely necessary for this game, but it makes for more lively play. You can just use your hands as a pretend crocodile.

Variations

- Substitute other animals and habitats for the crocodile. For example, try Bear in the Forest/Bear in the Cave; Lion on the Savannah/Lion in the Den.
- During quiet times, explain that crocodiles can be seen both on land and in water, look at pictures of these reptiles, and sing "The Crocodile Song."

Walk the Plank

Materials
Masking tape

Place a masking tape line on the floor. Pretend that the floor is the sea. See if your toddler can "walk the plank" (stay on the tape) without falling into the sea.

Variation
Create the plank with your child. Use a strip of cardboard or paper as a plank, and decorate it together with crayons or markers.

 Be careful anytime your child uses art supplies. Although nontoxic, crayons and marker caps are choking hazards. Stick with the "chunky" crayons (easier for little hands to hold, too) and remove the caps from the area. Even if you use "safety" markers (markers with specially designed caps that do not restrict airflow if they lodge in a child's throat), it's still a good idea to remove the caps from sight and reach of your little one.

Stepping Stones

Materials

Masking tape

Another fun imaginary water game is to walk or jump across "stepping stones." Make a series of lines or crosses on the floor with masking tape. Hop from tape to tape with your toddler. You can pretend you're hopping across a raging river. Do you see those crocodiles?

Variations

- If your child's name begins with an "I," "L," "T," "V," or "X," form that letter with the tape instead of a line or a cross.
- You can also make stepping stones from pieces of cardboard or paper. Before you play, tape them to the floor with masking tape. These stepping stones can be more easily rearranged in new patterns.

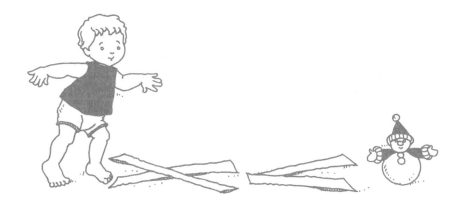

Circle Games

Materials
None

Simple word-and-action games expose toddlers to music as well as help them to build vocabulary and refine listening and motor skills. And, because the circle made by you and your child is small, you can play these games indoors as well as at the park. Be aware, however, that toddlers need lots of guidance to play these games.

- A good one to start with is "Ring Around the Rosie." After a few tries, most toddlers get into the "all fall down" part. (If you add the second verse, which ends, "We all stand up," this game will also help teach that concept.)
- Another great toddler tune is "This is the Way [We Bake the Bread, Early in the Morning]." Change the words to simple actions your toddler can mimic: for example, "This is the way we clap our hands . . . wave hello/goodbye . . . stamp our feet . . . swing our arms."

  Don't worry if you only know two or three circle games; toddlers thrive on repetition. And no matter what you sing, don't forget to clap after a song is finished. Your child will love being applauded.

Variations
- Adapt "Rosie" to other songs: No matter what song you sing, simply "all fall down" at the end.
- Next time you're outside with others, try the toddler version of "Duck-Duck-Goose." One child walks around the circle of children, tagging each one either a duck or a goose. However, because turn-taking is *not* something toddlers do best, when the "It" child says "Goose," let all the toddlers jump up and run!

Stop and Go

Materials

None

This is a fun way to work on coordination, help your child learn to follow directions and—best of all—facilitate naptime.

You and your toddler choose an action such as running, hopping, twisting or dancing. When you shout, "Go!" do the action. When you shout, "Stop!" freeze in place.

You will most likely have to demonstrate the game at least once and play it a few times before your child catches on.

If your child is like mine, she will be better at "going" than "stopping." We now play our own version of this game: When I say "Go!" he runs; when I say "Stop!" he says "No!," giggles, and keeps on running.

Variations

- Once you've played this game a while, try it with music. Use humming at first, or even playing random notes on a piano, if you have one handy. When you feel brave, try using a CD or tape (assuming you can safely lock away the equipment when the game is over, to avoid toddler electronic experimentation).
- Exchange the "Stop" and "Go" commands for other pairs. Here are some suggestions: fast and slow, loud and soft, noise and quiet.

Toddler Musical Chairs

Materials

Stereo and tape or CD

Let your child march in a circle while you sing, hum or play a tape or CD of music he likes. Stop the music and encourage him to sit down. Re-start the music and begin marching again. (Be prepared to do a lot of coaching.)

Variation

Play this game outside with a sprinkler. Turn the water on and march, dance, jump or run around. Turn the water off and stop, freeze or sit on the ground.

Marching Band/Parade

Materials
Pot lids
Paint stirrers (unused)
Wooden spoons
Coffee cans or oatmeal containers
Cardboard tubes

Transform everyday items into portable instruments. Paint stirrers make rhythm sticks, pot lids and wooden spoons are cymbals, soup pots are bass drums, coffee cans and oatmeal containers can be snare drums and cardboard tubes become horns or megaphones.

Avoid pot lids with thin edges. A toddler can hit himself with the lid and get cut.

Variation
Add melody to the parade by humming, singing or playing a tape or CD. Recordings allow you to introduce your toddler to different kinds of music.

Toddler Orchestra

Materials
*Laundry baskets, popcorn cans,
 coffee tins or oatmeal
 containers*
*Wooden spoons, plastic cooking
 utensils or cardboard tubes*
Tape

Household items can also be
used as instruments. Empty
cardboard tubes make great horns.
Overturned laundry baskets make great drum
sets. So do those large popcorn cans, if you can stand the sound.
And a few coffee cans or oatmeal containers taped together make
reasonably convincing bongo drums.

Let your toddler experiment with the different sounds made by a
variety of "drumsticks" (wooden spoons, plastic cooking utensils,
hands).

Variation
Extend the "musical" activities by decorating the drums, sticks and
horns with paper or fabric scraps, crayons, markers, paints, stickers or
magazine pictures.

Toddler Tambourine

Materials
Paper plates
Popcorn kernels, dried beans,
uncooked rice or pasta
Funnel
Tape
Nontoxic markers, crayons, paint,
stickers, magazine pictures, colored glue

Increase your toddler's instrument inventory by making tambourines from paper plates.

Fold a paper plate in half and seal almost all the edges with tape. Before adding the last piece of tape, insert the funnel into the plate and spoon in some popcorn kernels, dried beans or uncooked rice or pasta. (My son thought spooning the beans into the funnel was the best part of the craft.)

Decorate the tambourine with paint, crayons, markers, stickers, magazine pictures, and/or colored glue.

Several cautions: First, watch your child around the art materials. Also, do not use staples to seal the tambourines; they can hurt an inquisitive toddler. Finally, keep your eyes on your child as she plays with the dry ingredients.

Variation
Punch holes along the rim of the paper-plate tambourine and thread yarn or ribbon through the holes. (I make three so we can practice counting, too). Place clear tape over the holes to keep rice and small beans from falling out.

Dance

Materials
None

Put on music your toddler likes and dance. Daily dance parties are not only fun, they help toddlers refine gross motor skills. Dancing also offers an opportunity to reinforce simple word-and-action combinations, as you call out "clap your hands!" and clap your hands, or "stamp your feet" as you stamp your feet, and so on. Older toddlers can practice running in place and standing on one leg.

Your toddler will find you doing "The Twist" especially entertaining.

Variations

- Dance with a favorite doll or stuffed toy.
- Dance like a bubble, a snowflake, the rain, the wind, a fairy, an elephant or a dinosaur.
- Dance on egg cartons or large packing bubbles and make them pop. Be careful to keep these items out of your toddler's mouth, though!
- Wave scarves, crepe paper or ribbon streamers while dancing.

Be careful with these materials. Scarves pose strangulation dangers. You might also want to wait until your child won't eat the crepe paper before letting him dance with it.

Box Cars and Castles

Materials

Large appliance or other boxes

Large appliance boxes make great imaginary playthings. They can be castles, playhouses, forts, bear caves and ocean liners.

If you don't have appliance boxes, other boxes also make good structures. For example, if you buy economy-size boxes of diapers, save the box. Moving boxes, copy machine paper boxes, toy boxes and even the boxes you can get free from the package store make great cars, tunnels and planes.

Help your toddler decorate the structure you choose to build. If you're building a

- **Castle:** Decorate the lid flaps on the box as doors and drawbridges.
- **House:** Make a welcome mat from craft paper, or make a paper-plate wreath and hang it on the door. Put your house number on the outside to teach your toddler his address.
- **Boat:** Make a flag or a pennant from colored paper, and hoist it up a yardstick or broom handle. Make portholes, dials and gauges from construction paper.

You will know your box structure has outlived its developmental usefulness when your toddler starts climbing on its roof to reach the bookshelves, stereo or television.

If you have to cut the boxes, use a utility knife. Just don't let your toddler see you doing it—she might want to imitate you.

Gather

Materials

Basket, bucket, old handbag or other container with handles
Items to be gathered, such as toys, blocks, plastic utensils, cups,
*   stuffed animals, kitchen towels*

Give your toddler a container with handles (a basket, a bucket, an
old handbag) and encourage him to gather treasures.

Let him gather items such as toys, blocks, plastic utensils, cups,
stuffed animals and kitchen towels. Then dump them on the floor,
sort them into piles and put them in other containers. You can even
make towers with them.

To help build vocabulary, talk to your child about the objects he
finds—their color, shape, sound, texture or use.

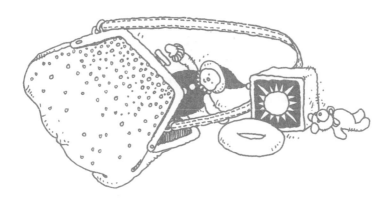

Hunt

Materials

Baskets, buckets, old handbags or other containers with handles

Items to be hunted, such as stuffed animals, toys, socks, kitchen
*   utensils*

This is like Gather (page 15), but instead of gathering random items, you and your child hunt for and collect specific objects. These can be any type of item (stuffed animals, toys or socks) or any theme (all red items, all holiday items or all square items).

Variations

- Make the items your child will find. For example, cut circles, flowers, hearts or worms out of construction paper. You could also make animal (or other) flashcards by gluing magazine pictures to lightweight cardboard.
- If your toddler is ready for a challenge, you can increase the learning value of this game by assigning her a specific goal: find only the blue cars, collect only three flowers or look only for triangles.

Match 'em Up

Materials
Shoes (4 to 6 pairs)
Socks (pairs)
Gloves (pairs)
Basket or bucket

Make a collection of four to six pairs of shoes, socks and gloves. Put one of each pair in a basket or bucket at one end of the room. Scatter the mates in plain sight at the other end of the room. Draw an item from the bucket and encourage your toddler retrieve its mate.

Variation
As your child gets better at this game, change the way he collects the items: Show him a picture of a shoe rather than giving him a shoe. Don't show him anything; instead, try speaking directions, such as, "Go get a shoe," or "Go get a blue mitten."

Alphabet Match

Materials

Plastic (refrigerator magnet)
    letters and numbers
Index cards with matching letters
    and numbers written on them
Markers

Show your toddler an index card with a letter or number on it and
have her retrieve the matching plastic version.

You might want to limit the selection, at least at first, to 1, 2, 3,
A, B, C, and the first letter of your child's name. (I also make the
card in colors to match the plastic letter; for example, if the plastic
"A" is red, I make a red "A" on the card.)

Variation

Not ready for letters? Show your child a picture of a bear, dog, bunny,
car or truck, and have her retrieve the matching stuffed animal or toy.

Soft Toss

Materials

Laundry basket, old drawer or large pot
Beanbag toys, soft dolls, rolled up socks or wadded up pieces of
paper

Help your child improve coordination by setting up a toss game with a laundry basket, old drawer or large pot. Using an underhanded throw, show him how to aim and toss beanbag toys, soft dolls, rolled-up socks or wadded up pieces of paper into the basket. Very young toddlers can walk to the basket and drop in the beanie.

 Do not use newspaper because the ink "offsets" onto your hands. Toddlers should not put that ink into their mouths.

Variations

- Do a theme toss by first Gathering (page 16) all the stuffed bunnies, rubber ducks or whatever you have three or four of. Pretend the basket is their "hole," "pond" or "cave," and toss the animals in.
- Hold up a hula-hoop and have your toddler toss the rolled up socks through the hoop. (Pretend the lions are jumping through fire at a circus.)

Ball Play

Materials
Lightweight vinyl ball
Oatmeal container
Small, lightweight basket

Because balls bounce, roll and in other ways escape, playing with them requires real coordination. Practice rolling first. Later try throwing and catching balls with your child to help develop gross motor skills. When you think your child is ready, try these fun ball games:

- **Play "hand golf"**: Make a tunnel with an oatmeal container by knocking out its bottom. Roll the ball through the tunnel at close range and again from farther away.
- **Play "crab trap"**: Have your youngster drop a lightweight basket over a rolling ball. This is good for hand-eye coordination.

Avoid foam or "stress" balls. They will break into small, swallowable pieces if chewed. Good balls for toddlers are small, about four inches in diameter, and a bit underinflated. Balls with too much "bounce" are hard to catch.

Toddler Bowling

Materials

Small, lightweight vinyl ball

Empty soda bottles, plastic containers, empty boxes or cardboard tubes

Have your child "bowl" by rolling (throwing, in my house) a small, lightweight ball at a grouping of light objects. These can be stacked plastic containers, empty soda bottles, empty boxes or even cardboard tubes stood on end.

Variations

- Let your toddler use a crumpled paper ball and walk up to the pins to knock them down.
- Make (or decorate) the bowling pins. Draw faces on the plastic bottles, and decorate the cardboard tubes with paint, markers or stickers.

Again, be aware of the choking dangers of markers and stickers, and do not allow your child to ingest paint, nontoxic though it may be.

Blankie Parachute

Materials
Small blanket, bath towel or pillowcase
Small, lightweight vinyl balls, teddy bear, rolled socks

Have some of the fun of gym-class parachuting at home with a small blanket, pillowcase or bath towel.

You and your toddler can each hold an end of the blanket and toss a teddy bear into the air. Or place five or six balls in the middle of the blanket and shake-shake-shake them out. With another adult, you can even lift the blanket up high so your toddler can run under it.

Toddler Ring Slide

Materials
Plastic curtain rings
Broom handle, rolling pin, cardboard tube or stool

Help your toddler slide plastic curtain rings over a broom handle, rolling pin, cardboard tube or the legs of an overturned stool. Help her slide them off again and then back on.

Variation
You and your toddler can make sliding rings by cutting a cardboard tube into slices and decorating with paint, glue or stickers.

CHAPTER 2

In the KITCHEN

These activities are some of my favorites. Each is based on edible materials, there's no preparation required— and you probably already have everything you need.

When doing some of these activities, protect your kitchen counter or table with used wrapping paper, waxed paper or cut-open shopping bags.

For extra-messy times, lay a shower curtain or newspapers under the work area to simplify clean-up.

Toddler Glitter

Materials
Sugar or salt
Food coloring
Plastic spice containers
Rice (optional)

Traditional glitter is definitely not for toddlers, so make some they can use. Fill a spice container with sugar, add a few drops of coloring, secure the lid and shake vigorously. If you live in a damp climate, add some grains of uncooked white rice to absorb the excess moisture and ensure smooth sprinkling.

Use Toddler Glitter alone (my son loves sprinkling it onto paper) or as a decoration for another project.

Before trying this activity, make sure your child is not allergic to food coloring.

Toddler Sand Art

Materials
Toddler Glitter (page 26)
Funnel
Pitcher
Clear plastic containers
Plastic spoons or scoops

Make two or three batches of Toddler Glitter. Using a funnel and a pitcher, fill recycled plastic containers with layers of glitter. Show your toddler how the different colors make different layers.

Variation
You can make gifts with sand art by pouring the different colors into cute plastic containers, such as the plastic bears that honey comes in.

Toddler Finger Paint

Materials

Applesauce
Waxed paper, craft paper or flattened paper bags
Food coloring (optional)
Flour, Toddler Glitter (page 26), raisins or other edible decorations

Even the youngest toddler can have safe finger-licking fun by
painting with applesauce on craft paper or opened-out paper bags. If
your child is not allergic to food coloring, add a few drops to the
applesauce to make different colors for him to explore.

Dress up your creations by sprinkling them with flour, Toddler
Glitter or edible decorations. You can also try adding a small amount
of cinnamon.

This activity also encourages toddlers to use all their senses:
feeling the substance, hearing its squishy sound, tasting and smelling
it as well as seeing the beautiful art they have created.

Unfortunately, the finished art will not keep long, so don't give
it to Grandma as a keepsake!

Jam Blob

Materials

Jam or jelly
Waxed paper
Spoon

Spoon some of your child's favorite jam onto a piece of waxed paper. Lay another piece of waxed paper on top, and have your child rub the jam with a spoon. The jam should squash down and spread, making an interesting blob picture. For a more interesting result, use more than one flavor or color of jam.

Variation

Make blobs with gelatin. Gelatin will not flatten the way jam does, and your toddler can have fun "chasing" the wiggly substance all over (or should I say, under) the waxed paper.

Mushy Mess

Materials

Prepared gelatin or pudding
Waxed paper, craft paper, flattened paper bags or plastic
(to cover table)
Plastic spoons or scoops (optional)
Plastic containers (optional)
Raisins, fruit pieces or cooked macaroni (optional)

Cover the kitchen table with plastic, paper bags or waxed paper. Drop a blob of gelatin or pudding on the paper and let your toddler explore squishing it around, "finger painting" with it or moving it from one plastic container to another with a spoon or scoop.

You can add texture to the pudding mush by including some raisins, cooked macaroni or pieces of fruit.

Toddler Jewelry

Materials

Pretzel rings, loop cereals or pasta
Yarn, ribbon or edible shoestring licorice

Both boys and girls enjoy making necklaces and bracelets by "stringing beads." This activity helps develop their fine motor skills.

For beads, I prefer to use edible items, because most toddlers still put everything in their mouths. Besides, the "beads" can double as snacks.

Check your cupboards: Pretzel rings and loop cereals work best. Dry pasta—such as wagon wheels, rigatoni or ziti—will also work, though it doesn't make much of a snack.

Help your toddler string these "beads" on yarn or ribbon.

Variation

You can introduce the idea of "sorting" by helping your child put the different "beads" into piles or containers.

Ice Painting

Materials
White paper
Drink mix powder
Ice cubes
Popsicle or ice cube trays (optional)
Popsicle sticks (optional)
Food coloring (optional)

Make a mound of drink mix powder on a large sheet of white paper. Let your child drag, rub, push and pull an ice cube through the pile. When she is finished, let the paper dry. It will be a wonderful ice painting!

Variation
You can also ice paint using a "paint Popsicle," which is frozen, food coloring-tinted water. The best way to make a paint Popsicle is to freeze colored water in Popsicle molds. If you have trouble finding these molds, you can also use ice cube trays. Place a wooden Popsicle stick in the middle of the cube before it freezes completely so your child will have something to hold.

Groovy Napkins

Materials

Plastic containers
Food coloring or gelatin (two or three different colors)
Paper napkins

In separate plastic containers, mix different colors of food coloring or gelatin with hot tap water. Fold and dip paper napkins into each color for a 1960s tie-dye look. Let the napkins air dry.

Larger, more expensive white dinner napkins work best for this activity. Keep in mind that although they are pretty at first, Groovy Napkins will get increasingly gross the longer they are saved, so do not plan to keep them around for too long.

If you choose to use gelatin, stir it frequently to keep it from setting.

Gelatin Soft Sculpture

Materials

Gelatin

Raisins or fruit pieces

Here is something to do with the gelatin left over from your Groovy
Napkin project (page 33). By the time you've finished, the gelatin
will probably be close to setting. Pour the gelatin into a clear
container and decorate it by dropping pieces of fruit or raisins into it.
You may also want to chill it the rest of the way and admire it some
more.

I don't really recommend eating this. If your child is like
mine, the gelatin won't be fit for human consumption after
either of these activities.

Egg Decoration

Materials
Hard-boiled eggs
Small sponge or sponge piece
Food coloring
Small plastic cup

Toddlers can decorate eggs safely without getting near boiling water by sponging on food coloring.

First, mix the food coloring with just a little water. (If you use too much water, the color will wash out and run off the egg.) Dip a small sponge (one-quarter of an ordinary cellulose sponge is the perfect size) into the food coloring. Apply the color to the egg.

Beware: This is *very* messy. Luckily, food coloring will wash out—eventually.

Make Colors

Materials
Plastic sandwich bags
Non-dairy topping
Food coloring
Tape

Fill a plastic sandwich bag with non-dairy topping and add a few drops of food coloring. Zip the bag closed and seal it well with tape. Have your toddler squeeze and knead the bag to turn the white foam into a pretty color.

Variation
Give your toddler a bag with two pre-mixed foam-colors. Let him knead them into a third color. Try red and blue (to make purple), blue and yellow (to make green), or red and yellow (to make orange).

Kitchen Water Play

Materials
Child-safe dishes, pots and flatware
Sponge, washcloth or soft-bristled brush
Plastic dishpan or large pot (optional)

This activity is best done in the summer because toddlers (and parents) are sure to get soaked. It also requires constant supervision, especially if your toddler is standing on a chair or stool by the sink.

Every toddler loves to wash the dishes. In the sink, or even at the table, fill a plastic dishpan or large pot with warm water. (Don't use soapsuds if your child will try to drink the water, as my son does!)

Equip your toddler with a sponge, washcloth or soft-bristled brush, and let him "wash" all the child-safe dishes in the house.

Variation
Let your toddler dip sponges in water and squeeze the water into cups, bowls and other containers.

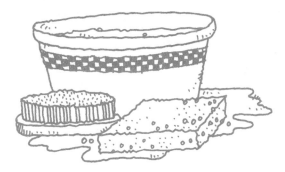

Personal Cabinet

Materials
Plastic containers and cups
Dried beans, uncooked rice or pasta

A Personal Cabinet is great for your toddler to have when you're working in the kitchen and he wants to be there with you. Pick one cabinet your toddler can reach (as far away from the stove as possible) and fill it with things that are safe and educational for toddlers. For example:

- **Containers:** Include a set of plastic containers or cups in graduated sizes that your toddler can "nest" and stack. Constructing stacks of containers and handling objects of different sizes and shapes helps your toddler develop problem-solving, spatial relations and other important pre-math skills.
- **Shakers:** Shakers also provide fun learning opportunities. Your toddler will learn about different noises and cause and effect: when this is shaken, it makes a sound. You can make your own shakers by filling small containers with beans, rice or pasta. Be sure the lids cannot be removed, though, as your toddler is sure to try to find out what's inside.

Variation

You and your toddler can make shakers as an art project. Before filling the container, decorate it with crayons, markers, paints, magazine pictures, paper, fabric scraps, Toddler Glitter (page 26) or colored glue.

Peanut Butter Fun Dough

Materials

Peanut Butter
Honey
Powdered Milk

Dough is a wonderful substance for toddlers. There's no "one right way" to play with it, and dough helps fuel your child's imagination as he devises new things to do with (and to) it.

There are many dough recipes using all kinds of products, but because toddlers put things in their mouths, most are better saved for a later age. Try the following simple recipe:

Peanut Butter Dough

1 part smooth peanut butter (not crunchy)
1 part honey
2 parts dry milk powder

Mix all the ingredients in a bowl. If necessary, adjust quantities to make a workable dough.

This is an easy recipe, so you and your child can concoct it together. He can scoop and pour ingredients from one container to another while you talk about the ingredients, their texture and the measurements.

More than just edible, the dough is downright tasty, so it doubles as a snack. However, it does not keep very long or air-dry satisfactorily.

- This peanut butter dough is useful *only* if your child is not allergic to peanut butter itself.
- Do not use chunky peanut butter, as nuts are considered choking hazards all through the toddler years.
- Remember also that children under age one should not eat honey.
- If your child is allergic to powdered milk, substitute flour for a slightly less tasty dough.

Variation

For even tastier and more nutritious dough, substitute one part oatmeal for one part of the dry milk. (This is the preferred version at our house.)

Dough Play

Materials

Peanut Butter Fun Dough (*page 40*)
Cookie cutters, plastic puzzle pieces, leaves or flowers,
     containers, toy cars and animals, sticks, spoons (optional)

Dough play is open-ended, and there are lots of things to do with it.
For example:

- Young toddlers can simply explore (and eat) it. They can roll it,
  press it, pinch it, pound it and squeeze it.
- Flatten it with a rolling pin.
- Make balls, ropes and braids.
- Experiment with impressions: press into it with
  cookie cutters, plastic puzzle pieces, leaves and/or
  flowers, the top of the sippy cup or an empty
  plastic container or lid.

- Make tracks on the dough with a toy car or plastic animal.
- "Draw" on a dough pancake with a twig, plastic spoon or baby fork.
- Fill a cookie cutter or small cup with tiny dough balls.
- Make dough food (cookies, eggs, pies and cakes are fun) and serve it on plastic plates.

If you keep your dough-play equipment in a large plastic container or coffee can, you won't have to search the kitchen for them every time you make fun dough.

Variations

For variety, add salt, sugar, dry oatmeal or cornmeal to some of the dough. Discuss the new textures these new ingredients make.

Your toddler can also decorate her dough creations. Use raisins, rice, dried beans, seeds, barley, Toddler Glitter (page 26), pretzels, breakfast cereal or anything else on hand that's edible.

Shortbread Cookies

Materials

Butter, margarine or shortening
White flour
Sugar
Salt
Toddler Glitter (page 26), sprinkles, chips or other edible
    decorations

If you want to make dough as an activity itself, I recommend this simple shortbread recipe. There are no eggs in shortbread, which makes the dough safer to sample while it is raw. What toddler can resist tasting dough?

Also, shortbread dough has to be refrigerated before it can be shaped into cookies. That means that by the time your toddler's attention span has run its course, you are finished with Phase One: making the dough. Later, when you are both ready, you and your toddler can turn to Phase Two: shaping and decorating. (I've waited as long as a week before my son felt like baking again.)

After you have formed the cookies, cover the cookie sheet with plastic and refrigerate. Bake the cookies while your child naps.

The recipe is short and simple:

Basic Shortbread

1 cup butter, margarine or shortening
2 cups flour
$\frac{1}{2}$–$\frac{3}{4}$ cup sugar
$\frac{1}{2}$ teaspoon salt

In a mixing bowl, beat the butter and sugar. Add flour and salt. Wrap the dough in plastic or store in an airtight container in refrigerator for at least two hours before using.

Form the dough into cookies, decorate to your liking and bake at 375° for about 15 minutes on an ungreased cookie sheet.

Variations

Use shortbread dough to make handprint cookies. Roll out the dough to about ½-inch thickness and cut out a circle. Firmly press your child's hand onto the dough and then remove his hand immediately before he can make a fist or otherwise destroy the imprint.

- Use colored sugar or other decorations to fill in the impression of your child's hand.
- Dip your little one's hand in warm water, then colored sugar, and then onto the cookie.
- Use a plastic knife to stipple the outline of your child's hand on the dough and cut out the hand shape.

This activity comes with the usual cautions about using a hot oven. Either bake the cookies while your child naps, or put a safety gate between him and the oven.

Handprint cookies are a difficult project. You may have to do a lot of persuading and directing to get the hand positioned correctly onto the cookie. Be prepared to downsize your gift plans. Consider the project successful if it results in one beautifully wrapped cookie for each set of grandparents.

Cookie-Dough Cookies

Materials

Store-bought roll of cookie dough

*Toddler Glitter (page 26), sprinkles, chips, or other edible
    decorations*

The easiest way to make cookies with toddlers is with a store-bought
roll of cookie dough. This lets you get right to the decorating part
without the delay of having to make the dough. For decorations, try
tinted sugar, cinnamon candies, raisins, sprinkles or chips. You can
also use Toddler Glitter, provided you've made it with sugar rather
than salt.

Read the ingredients on the package to make sure there
aren't any substances in the product that your child may be
allergic to.

Flour Play

Materials
Flour
Measuring spoons, cups, ladles
Coffee can
Dry oatmeal, cornmeal, cereal
(optional)

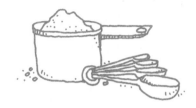

Set out a pile of flour on the kitchen table. Provide measuring spoons, cups and ladles. Your toddler can play "chemist" by moving flour from container to container, "baker" by spooning flour into a measuring cup, or she can just enjoy the sensation of playing with the stuff Mommy and Daddy bake with!

Store the flour in an old coffee can for repeat uses.

Variations

- Provide her with some other substances to explore along with the flour, such as dry oatmeal, cornmeal or cereal.
- Show her what happens when you add water to the flour.

Sort Silverware

Materials

Silverware

If your child can identify forks, knives and spoons, you can introduce sorting skills. Have him sort the clean dinner knives, spoons and forks into the cutlery drawer.

This activity is really for the nearly-three set. Supervise closely, because knives and forks are involved.

Kitchen Sensory Adventure

Materials

"Smell" food, such as vinegar, garlic, peanut butter or cloves
"Taste" food, such as plain yogurt, chocolate or salty crackers
"Touch" food, such as applesauce, jam, oatmeal or cooked rice

Put out three or four items for your toddler to taste, smell or touch. Stick with one sense at a time, and use foods that feel or taste quite different from one another. Describe the experience to your toddler, using as many words as you can to help build her vocabulary.

Sandwich Geometry

Materials
Sandwich

When you feed your toddler a sandwich, teach her some pre-math.
Cut the sandwich into two halves or rectangles, four squares or
quarters or two or four triangles. Explain to your child what you are
doing. When she has enough language skills to answer you, start
asking her whether she wants two or four pieces, triangles or
rectangles.

Milk Voilà!

Materials
Food coloring
Milk

If your child has no allergies to milk or food coloring, try this lunchtime surprise. Put two or three drops of food coloring in the bottom of a plastic cup. Add milk, and *voilà!* Colored milk! It's simple, and your child will love it.

CHAPTER 3

In the DINING ROOM

The following activities emphasize thinking skills, fine motor coordination and language development.

In truth, you don't actually need to use the dining room. A table just about anywhere will do. I always use the dining room, because with a toddler around, we just don't do that much formal dining these days.

Toddler Confetti

Materials
Magazines, construction paper, junk mail or old wrapping paper

Here is a way for your child to both develop fine motor skills and vent frustrations. Give her a pile of magazines, construction paper, junk mail or old wrapping paper and let her tear it, poke holes in it and otherwise manipulate it.

 Avoid newspaper because its ink rubs off easily.

Variations
- Your child can fill a box or make a pile of her confetti.
- Sprinkle the confetti on a cookie sheet and show your child how to "write" in it. Make individual letters and spell out her name.
- Use confetti to decorate boxes or other items, or to make collage pictures or greeting cards.

Toddler Origami

Materials

Aluminum foil

Paper napkins, paper towels, junk mail, construction paper

Let your child play with foil, folding, pressing and straightening it out again. Foil is easy to manipulate.

Then let your toddler try folding paper napkins, paper towels, junk mail flyers and other kinds of paper. This activity helps develop fine motor coordination as well as introduces rudimentary concepts (change, cause and effect).

Keep the foil box, with its sharp cutting edge, away from your toddler. Also, watch that he doesn't fold these paper products into such small pieces that he's tempted to eat them. Don't use newspaper.

Treasure Dig

Materials

Shirtbox or other carton
Shredded paper, cotton balls or fabric scraps
Vinyl snakes, beanie animals, plastic letters or other small fun
*   surprises*
Plastic spoons and/or cup (optional)

Lay an assortment of fun surprises in the bottom of a box and cover them with shredded paper, cotton balls or fabric scraps.

Help your child find her surprises by "digging" with a plastic spoon, a cup or her hands.

The surprises can be just about anything, from small toys to brightly colored refrigerator magnets. (My son likes finding snakes and then examining them with a plastic magnifying glass.)

Surprise Box

Materials

Shoebox, wipes box or other easy-to-open container
Greeting cards, playing cards, postcards, photos, scraps of fabric,
*   magazine pictures, masking tape and other fun objects*

Help your child develop her coordination by playing the toddler favorite, "dump and fill." (I should warn you, it's mostly "dump" at my house.)

Find a container he can open himself, such as a shoebox, wipes box or large cup with a lid, and fill it with "surprises"—greeting cards, playing cards, postcards, photos, magazine pictures, fabric, masking tape, blocks, balls or other toys. You can use just about anything you can think of—it's all new and fascinating to your toddler.

Encourage your child's language development by talking to him about the objects in the box. Say their names, colors, shapes, the sounds they make and what they are used for.

Variation

Choose a theme for the box. For example, sharpen your toddler's sense of touch by filling the box with a variety of textures from your ragbag and toolbox (soft satin, rough corduroy or scratchy sandpaper). Or, he can experiment with sounds in a box filled with noisemakers (the rattles and other "noisy" toys you already have); explore round objects with a box of balls, oranges and apples or make friends with a collection of farm animals.

To give your toddler freedom to explore the items on his own, do not include any objects that will slide through a toilet paper tube and thus be a choke hazard.

The Feel-y Game

Materials

Box, bag or pillowcase

*Common objects such as a baby bottle, a ball, a spoon, a plastic
mug, a board book or a rubber duck*

This is a good activity for stimulating your child's tactile senses,
developing thinking skills and building vocabulary.

Put into the box, bag or pillowcase some objects that your toddler
can easily recognize, such as a baby bottle, ball, spoon, plastic mug,
rubber duck, favorite toy, board book, sippy cup, rattle or thick crayon.

Ask your child to put his hand in and identify what he feels
without looking at the object.

This can be a pretty difficult game for a young toddler. Have
fun with it and don't expect too much from your child.

Remember to avoid using choke hazards — objects that slide
through a cardboard tube.

Variation

To increase the tactility of this
game, glue different textures
(rough burlap, smooth
rayon, bumpy seeds pasted
onto paper) onto the box
walls. Your child can help
with this.

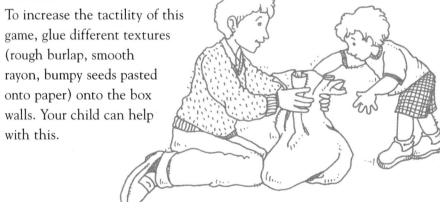

Exploration Center

Materials

Cardboard egg carton

Dried beans, cotton, feathers, ribbon, stones, bark, acorns,
material scraps and other interesting items

Glue (optional)

Help your toddler fill each cup of a cardboard (not Styrofoam) egg carton with a variety of interesting items. Glue them in place if you want to (or if it helps to keep your child from eating them). Some suggestions: bark (found on the ground, not stripped from the tree); acorns; dried beans; cotton; candy; dirt; material scraps such as burlap, velvet, corduroy and silk; pasta (uncooked); pinecones, pom-poms; ribbon; rice; sandpaper; sponge bits and stones.

Talk to your toddler about these items, exposing him to as rich and varied a vocabulary as you can.

 Because many of these items are small, you need to closely supervise your toddler during this activity. Gluing the items in place will help minimize the chance that he will put them into his mouth.

Variation

Make an exploration box based on the ABCs. Fill each cup with items beginning with a letter of the alphabet. Do this in ABC order. "A" is for aluminum foil or acorns, "B" is for beans or burlap, "C" is for cotton or cranberries. Or spell out your child's name: "T" is for tinfoil or tapestry, "E" is for envelope or earth and "D" is for dental floss or dandelions.

Toddler Counters

Materials

Muffin pan

Your toddler's favorite snack (cereal, pretzel loops, raisins)

Emphasize counting and fine motor skills with this activity. Help your
two-year-old count out and distribute a favorite snack into the muffin
cups (eating as she goes) in quantities of one to six. One cup holds
one item, the next cup holds two items, the next three, and so on up
to six.

Use whatever snack your toddler prefers—larger ones such as
pretzel loops or animal crackers are easiest for toddlers to manipulate.
Loop cereals and raisins will also work.

Variation

If your toddler doesn't feel like counting, try simple identification.
Ask her to hand you one pretzel, or the yellow loop or the lion
cracker.

Pick Up Blocks

Materials
Tongs
Muffin tins
Blocks or large pegs

This early motor coordination game requires your toddler to use the tongs to manipulate items. Place a block or peg in half the cups of the muffin pan. Have your child grab an item with the tongs and move it from one cup to another, or from one cup to the table and back.

Variation
Help your toddler with language by speaking directions to her: ask her to pick up the red peg or the green block. Ask her to move two blocks to the table.

Circles and Squares

Materials

A *round container, such as a cottage cheese or dessert topping container*

A *rectangular container, such as a shoebox*

Round and square objects such as pegs, wood blocks, plastic blocks or coasters

Help your child sort square objects (blocks) into the square container and round objects (plastic pegs) into the round container.

Once she masters this, have her sort only the round (or square) objects by characteristics such as color and size. For example, sort the square blocks by size into two square boxes, one larger than the other. Similarly, she can sort the round pegs by color into two round containers, one red and one blue.

Sorting games help develop pre-math and pre-reading skills. Sort by only one characteristic (size, color, shape) at a time to avoid confusing your child.

If your child will try to eat the beans or stick them up her nose, use cereal.

Variations

• Sort a small pile of beans, pasta and/or cereal by type, color or size.

• Try sorting socks. You will have to limit the selection and choose pairs that are obviously different from one another—a black pair, a red-striped pair, a white tube sock, a small blue one. (I'll let you know when I've figured out how to actually get help with the laundry using this game.)

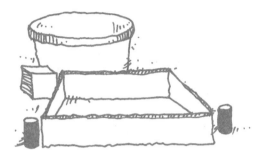

Tabletop Sorting

Materials

Plastic containers or
muffin tin
Magazine pictures

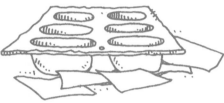

Rather than sorting three-dimensional objects, use paper ones. Cut out various magazine pictures of animals, vehicles or other subjects. Set out a few plastic containers or a muffin tin and your pile of magazine pictures. Together, separate dogs from cats, cars from trucks, flowers from butterflies. As you separate the pictures, put them in their own container or section.

Variations

• Make and decorate the paper shapes with your toddler. Cut out circles and squares from construction paper, wrapping paper or other paper or cardboard. Adorn with markers, paints, crayons, Toddler Glitter (page 26) or Toddler Confetti (page 54).

• Play a holiday sorting game using appropriate shapes such as flags, turkeys or pumpkins. Make them yourself, or use stickers, wrapping paper and magazine images.

If you make the sorting shapes yourself, watch your toddler closely to be sure the paints go on the paper and not in your child's mouth. Minimize choking dangers by using chunky crayons and removing the marker caps from the table.

Animal Habitats

Materials

Construction paper or posterboard
Magazine cutouts
Glue

On a piece of construction paper or posterboard, sketch a ranch-style fence to indicate a farm, a series of boxes to represent the zoo or a grouping of thick and thin lines to signify a forest or jungle.

Then, spread an assortment of magazine cutouts or stickers on the table. Help your child select the pictures of animals and glue them to the drawings of their correct habitats.

Variations
- Draw a rectangle to represent a suitcase. Sort only images of clothes and shoes.
- Draw a simple house outline. Have your child select only furniture cutouts. If this is too easy for her, divide the big house into one or two (or more) "rooms" such as kitchen and bathroom. Help her to put the appropriate furnishings or utensils into their proper room.

Although glue sticks are neater than liquid glue, they can be very dangerous for toddlers. Both the sticks and the caps pose choking hazards.

Picture Book

Materials
Magazines, postcards,
    old calendars, stickers
Scissors
Construction paper
Glue
Ribbon or yarn
Hole punch
Markers, crayons or paint

With your toddler, hunt through magazines, calendars and postcards for pictures of animals, babies, cars-any item you know he can recognize. As you find them, cut out the pictures and set them aside. Depending on your child, you may want to rip out the pages first and use scissors later.

At the table, make a booklet by gluing the pictures on several pieces of construction paper. Bind the book by punching holes and having your toddler thread ribbon or yarn through. He can decorate the cover with markers, crayons, paint or other art materials.

Supervise your child carefully with art supplies and glue. Gluesticks are not recommended for toddlers.

Matching Cards

Materials

Index cards, posterboard or thin cardboard
Scissors
Pairs of pictures from magazines, coloring books or wrapping paper

Lots of matching cards are available commercially, but they're really easy to make yourself, too. Purchase duplicate copies of magazines or coloring books, and cut out pairs of images from them. You can also find pairs of objects on the repeating pattern of most wrapping paper.

The objects pictured should be familiar to your toddler, such as triangles, cats, dogs, teddy bears.

Make the matching cards by gluing one image on one index card and its mate on another. (This is a fun project for you and your toddler in itself.)

To play the matching game, spread three to five matching pairs on the table and let your child match the sets.

Later, when he's mastered the concept, use the matching cards to play Concentration (also known as Memory). Turn the cards facedown on the table. Have your child turn over two cards. If they match, he has a set. If they do not match, he turns them facedown and tries again.

Variations

- Use identical sets of stickers to make matching cards.
- Rather than pasting pictures, use nontoxic markers to draw your own sets of circles, squares or diamonds.
- Use playing cards as matching sets. This helps expose your toddler to numbers, but make sure you select cards that are clearly different from one another.

Matching Columns

Materials

Construction (or other) paper
2 sets of identical stickers

Make a column of different stickers on one side of the paper. Let your child apply the matching stickers to the other side of the paper.

Because stickers tend to come in "sets," you can use this game to talk about classification. For example, a set of farm animal stickers allows you to talk about that habitat, and why some animals live there while others live in the forest or the jungle.

Matching Puzzles

Materials

Index cards, posterboard or thin cardboard

Glue

Scissors

Pairs of pictures from magazines, coloring books or wrapping paper

Start by gluing both matching images on the same rectangle. Then, cut the rectangle into two puzzle pieces. Cut on a slant, in a wavy line or on a curve. In any case, try to make unique cuts for each of matching mates so that your toddler can be certain she has fit the two together.

Variation

Instead of rectangles as the base shape, make two-piece puzzles in other shapes your toddler will recognize: squares, circles, stars. You can even make special holiday puzzles in the shape of hearts, eggs or pumpkins.

Cookie Cutter Matching

Materials
Cookie cutters
Construction paper
Marker

Sharpen your toddler's visual discrimination and problem-solving skills with this toddler classic. First, trace around three or four cookie cutters onto the construction paper. Then challenge your child to match the cookie cutter with its traced image.

Variations

- Instead of cookie cutters, use three plastic cups in graduated sizes. Trace around the cup and have your child match the cup with its corresponding circle. Talk about small, medium and large.
- Use plastic refrigerator magnet letters to trace your child's name. Have her match the letters with their tracing.

Toddler Puzzles

Materials
Large calendar or magazine picture
Cardboard
Glue
Scissors
Cereal or gift box (optional)

Let your child decorate a large paper shape and glue it to a square piece of cardboard. Then cut it into three or four pieces. Together, mix the pieces up and then reassemble them.

Variations
- An even faster way to make puzzles is to cut up a ready-made item with a picture already on it, such as a cereal or gift box.
- When she's ready, your toddler can make a more challenging puzzle. Instead of a square, make some other recognizable shape (a letter, a number or a heart) to decorate and cut into four to six pieces.

 Styrofoam trays are often cited as a great medium for homemade puzzles. Like many great craft ideas, this one won't work with toddlers. Styrofoam looks good enough to eat to most toddlers—and they will try!

CHAPTER 4

In the NURSERY

Here are some low-energy activities, many of them warm
and fuzzy, to help you bond with your toddler while having
some laughs and teaching some skills. If you're lucky, he
might even sit still for two, maybe even three minutes!

Toddler Weather Report

Materials

Magnetic board with magnets representing the sun and a rain cloud

As part of your morning routine, begin assessing the weather. Cut out a yellow sun and a blue cloud and glue them to magnets. You may have to be creative in finding a surface that will hold them; we use a small magnetic "cubby" board at my house.

Every morning, ask your toddler to go to the window and see if it is raining or not. If it is raining, she can put up the cloud magnet; if it is sunny, he can put the sun magnet up.

A chalkboard may seem an obvious alternative, but I avoid using chalk with toddlers because it should not be ingested.

Breakfast in Bed

Materials
Blanket
Plastic dishes and cups (optional)
Food, real or pretend

It's always fun to eat a real or pretend meal somewhere other than the kitchen table. Use portable breakfast food (cereal bars, jelly sandwiches, toaster tarts) or pretend food made from Peanut Butter Fun Dough (page 40). Spread a blanket on the bed or the floor.

Dresser-Drawer Costumes

Materials

Clothing, both yours and your child's

Costumes are great just to run around the house in. My son loves to wear his clown costume—only it's not a costume, just his own clothes: mismatched print pants and a print shirt, and two socks of different colors. Sometimes we embellish the outfit by adding a vest, one of my hats and a pair of my shoes and gloves. Gardening gloves, which are white, look pretty authentic. He also likes to put bandages on his face. He's also been known to put stickers on his cheeks.

Other dresser-drawer costumes include:

- **Chef:** white shirt and pants (we use this for baking).
- **Roman:** Daddy's white T-shirt, Mommy's green headband.
- **Surfer:** a bathing suit, complete with cardboard surfboard he decorated himself.
- **Painter:** An old, paint-stained shirt. (I confess. This one is really a trick I devised to minimize the clothes damaged by arts and crafts.)
- **Tarzan:** his very favorite costume. He gets to run around with no clothes on at all.

Dress Up

Materials

Adult shoes, hats, vests, scarves or necklaces

Admiring themselves in the mirror is always fun for toddlers. Make a collection of adult shoes, vests, hats, scarves and long necklaces—in other words, things a two-year-old can put on without assistance. Both boys and girls enjoy this kind of imitative and imaginary play, and they learn about dressing, too.

> Make sure you supervise this activity. Scarves and necklaces can be strangulation hazards.

Variation

As they get older, children like to play imaginative dress-up games, pretending to be different characters or professions, even acting out stories. You may want to enlarge your dress-up collection with some dollar-store items such as cowboy, firefighter or construction worker hats.

Clothes Matching

Materials

A basket of clothes

This game can be played with your collection of dress-up clothes or with the clean clothes in your laundry basket.

With the basket of clothes before you, ask your child to find specific articles of clothing, and praise her when she finds them in the basket and brings them to you. Ask her to find a yellow scarf, a black shoe, an undershirt or a pair of shorts. Have her find a hat that a cowboy, construction worker or firefighter would wear, a shoe to wear in the snow or one of her daddy's socks.

Count Buttons and Snaps

Materials

Your toddler's clothes

Introduce your toddler to numbers by making a counting game out of getting dressed. As you snap his pants, shirts or onezies, count "one snap, two snap," up to five. You can even sing songs about it. Instead of "One, Two, Buckle My Shoe," try "One, two, button your shirt."

Variations

- While you are dressing your toddler, talk to him about "right" and "left." As you put on his clothes, you can chant, "left foot, right foot, left hand, right hand." Try adapting the words to "Hokey Pokey." Sing, "you put your left leg in, you put your left leg in," as you put his left leg in his pants, and so on.
- Count other things in the nursery, such as books, toys, animals, shoes or photographs.

Count and Take

Materials

Small objects, such as toy animals, books, blocks or pegs

Count out 12 small objects into a pile between you and your toddler, counting out loud as you do so. Remove one and place it in front of you. Encourage your child to do the same. Now remove two and have her do the same. Alternate between one and two until all the items are gone.

Repeat the game if your toddler finds this interesting.

Don't forget to talk as you play, counting out loud and describing the items you are counting.

Variation

Play this game with edible items such as animal crackers, pretzels or loop cereals. When you remove an item from the pile, eat it!

Review the Baby Book

Materials
Baby book

My son loves looking at the little album that chronicles his first year. He enjoys identifying all the family members, and I enjoy the quiet time. Looking at photographs also provides a good opportunity to build vocabulary, talk about family relationships and introduce spatial concepts such as "behind" and "next to." For example: "Dustin is your cousin," "Pop-Pop is Mommy's Daddy," "Look! Who is sitting next to Baby Teddy?"

Countdown Chain

Materials

*Construction paper, junk mail or wallpaper samples, cut into
one- to two-inch strips*

Markers, crayons

Toddler Glitter (page 26) or Toddler Confetti (page 54) (optional)

Tape

Scissors

Cut a number of one- to two-inch strips, each about a foot long, from the paper, junk mail or wallpaper samples. Form the first link by taping the ends of the strip together to make a closed circle. Add the next link by threading the strip through the first loop before taping the ends together. Continue in this manner until you've made a chain of linked loops.

When completed, hang the chain on your child's wall, and let her pull off one link per day. This can be the start of a nice tradition at your house.

It is not necessary to spend a lot of time creating the chain; the main activity is pulling off one link per day. Don't fuss too much if your child wants to pull off more than one link at a time. She'll catch on eventually.

Tempting though it may be, don't use staples to fasten the links—children can get hurt when they pull on them. Use tape instead.

Variations

- Try letting your child decorate some of the links with markers, crayons, Toddler Glitter or Toddler Confetti.
- First make the "links" and then build the chain as you Hunt (page 16) for them.
- Make countdown chains for any holiday, from Halloween to your toddler's birthday. Adjust the colors, number of links and decorations accordingly.
- Write a message on the link for your toddler to find when he pulls it from the chain. Her name is always a good choice. So are holiday-related words ("BOO" is my favorite). Also try letters (A, B, C, the first letter of her name) and numbers (1, 2, 3).

Pick Out the "T"

Materials

Letters — refrigerator magnet letters, toy letters, letters cut from paper or letters in an alphabet book

Toddlers love to hear their own names and anything related to their own names as well. (My son Teddy has been saying, "T is for me," since he learned to speak.) Take advantage of this egocentrism to introduce your child to letters. Show her some letters, such as large plastic refrigerator magnet letters, large cutouts from magazines or even large letters in an alphabet book. Ask her to show you the first letter of her name.

Talk On the Phone

Materials

Toy or real phone

This is a good way to encourage verbal skills as well as to begin teaching your toddler her full name and phone number.

Use an old phone, disconnect your real one or try a toy phone. Pretend to dial, and then talk to Pop-Pop, Aunt Kathy, cousin Tina or a faraway Dustin.

Variation

Make your own phone with two paper (not Styrofoam) cups and two pieces of string. Decorate the cups, if you like, and then tape the string to the bottom to form the "cord."

To avoid strangulation dangers, make two separate phones and keep the "cord" string short.

Where Is Dolly?

Materials

Dolls, stuffed animals or beanies

"Where is Thumbkin?" may not be Grammy material, but young children love it. Change the words to help your toddler identify the toys and animals in her room. Ask "Where is Dolly?" or "Where is Rabbit?" As you sing the "Here I am" line, produce the named toy, making it bounce up and down, growl or give kisses.

Where is Thumbkin
Where is Thumbkin
Here I am, here I am
How are you today, sir?
Very well, I thank you,
Run away, run away.

Body Naming

Materials

None

Band-Aids (optional)

Here's a fun, loving way to review the parts of the body. Snuggle together. Ask your toddler to kiss your chin, forehead, nose, shoulder, hand. Reciprocate often.

Variation

Help your child put Band-Aids on her hand, knee or foot. Let her put Band-Aids on you. Use brightly colored children's bandages if you can get them; if you can't, good old beige ones are fine.

Because bandages are made for skin, these are a safer choice than stickers.

Box Zoo

Materials

Boxes, varied in size
Stuffed animals that fit in the boxes
Imagination

Together with your toddler, place the boxes about the room, and fill each one with a stuffed animal.

Pretend to be zookeepers and care for the animals, or pretend to be visitors touring the zoo. Talk about your animal collection: where each animal lives, how many legs it has, its color, its size or its eating and sleeping habits.

Variations

- Make a pet store. Pretend to feed and groom the animals and/or pretend to be customers looking for the perfect pet. Talk about which animals make good pets.
- Forget the boxes and make a jungle. Drape green crepe paper around the animals to represent jungle vines and overgrowth. Pretend you are on safari, seeking out the mighty lion. Talk to your child about which animals live in the jungle and which do not.

Practice Prepositions

Materials

A *favorite toy*

Here's a great activity for concept development and vocabulary building. Give your toddler his favorite toy, doll or stuffed animal. Demonstrate and then direct him to place it on, under, next to, in front of or behind the bed, a chair or a doorway.

Variations

- Ask your toddler to hand you something that is next to or behind something else.
- Place two or three toys, stuffed animals or dolls or books under the blanket or under the bed. Have your child retrieve them, emphasizing the concepts of "under," "appear" and "reappear."

Animal Matching

Materials

Children's books

Stuffed animals

Read an animal book such as, *Brown Bear, Brown Bear What Do You See?* or *I Went Walking,* or sing a song like "Old MacDonald Had a Farm." Have your toddler match the pictures or names of the animals on the page or in the song with animals from his stuffed toy collection.

How far you go with this activity depends on how many different animals you have in your house. Don't forget the rubber duckies in the bathroom!

Flashlight Game

Materials
Flashlight

Turn out the light in the toddler's room, and turn on the flashlight. Shine the flashlight on an object and name it, or ask your two-year-old to name it for you.

You can also use the flashlight to teach concepts such as dark and light, off and on and bright and dim.

Dino-Gone

Materials

Water

Food coloring (optional)

Lemon juice, spices, extracts (optional)

Plastic spray bottle

For some toddlers it's monsters. For my son, it's dinosaurs. Dinosaurs lurk on the dark stairs and in his empty bedroom. So I invented Dino-Gone.

Dino-Gone can be made as simply as filling a spray bottle with water; but making an activity out of it is lots more fun. Start with a plastic container of water. Add food coloring. Feel free to supply some mythology about the color—dinosaurs can't see red, or dinosaurs get sick when they see green.

Next, add something smelly, such as a few drops of lemon juice or a pinch of spice. Again, take liberties with the properties of these substances—lemons make dinosaur scales fall off or that cinnamon smells terrible to a dinosaur.

Stir the mixture well, mumble some magic words over the bowl and pour the whole mix into a dinosaur eliminator applicator (spray bottle).

To rid your house of dinosaurs, spray Dino-Gone under the bed, in the closet or wherever dinosaurs hide in your house. Usually, it's best to spray before bedtime. Repeated application may be necessary.

- Do not use glitter. It may make Dino-Gone pretty, but glitter is not a safe substance for toddlers.
- Don't spray any surface that could be harmed or stained by the ingredients in your Dino-Gone.

CHAPTER 5

In the BATHROOM

Bathtubs are for splashing—and what toddler doesn't love a good splash? But even the rest of the bathroom can be the site of some good clean fun with your toddler.

Break and Enter

Materials

Crepe paper streamers

Tape

Turn the bathroom doorway into a fun challenge for your toddler to enter. Tape one or two crepe paper streamers across the doorway that he can break through, crawl under or jump over.

Variations

- Cover the door with a whole sheet of thin paper for him to break into.
- Lay bubble wrap on the threshold for him to pop as he walks (or hops) over them.

Tiger Brushing

Materials

Toothbrush

Toothpaste (optional)

Next time you and your toddler are enjoying a toothpaste moment, try this game to help encourage her cooperation. Have her growl like a tiger (lips bared, teeth together). This puts the front teeth into position to be brushed. Next, have her open her mouth wide and roar like a lion; you can get at the tops and sides of the teeth.

When she turns into a frog, you can brush her long, sticky tongue, and she'll need to be an elephant to rinse and squirt all the water out of her mouth.

✻ Check with your dentist regarding the use of toothpaste and the proper brushing techniques for toddlers.

Play "Boo Boo"

Materials

Bandages, toilet paper, or Ace bandage

This is the toddler version of playing doctor: the patient needs bandaging! If you have some econo-bandages to spare, use them. If not, let your child bandage you with toilet paper or an Ace bandage.

Keep the Ace bandage clips away from your toddler; those small, sharp points can really hurt.

Bandage Un-Roll

Materials

Toilet paper or Ace bandage
Small surprises

During naptime, roll a small toy, block, note or treat (wrapped) in a length of toilet paper (or use an Ace bandage). Have your toddler unroll the paper to find his prize.

Again, if you use an Ace bandage, keep the clips away from your toddler.

Wash Puppets

Materials
Sock
Laundry marker

Put the sock over your hand and draw a face on it with a
laundry marker.

These puppets are fun and functional in the bath—they "kiss"
my son and clean his face! They also add some zest to the old
standards such as ,"Peek-a-Boo," "Pat-a-Cake,"
"Got Your Nose" and "This Little Piggy."

As your child gets older, the puppet
can help you read stories.

Bath Pictures

Materials

Sandwich-size plastic bags

Photographs, magazine pictures, colored paper shapes
or other art

Tape

Put together some waterproof pictures for the bath by encasing four
or five visuals in sandwich-size plastic bags. Use photographs,
magazine pictures or construction paper shapes. Seal the bags and
tape over the opening. During bathtime, you can talk to your child
about the pictures (who, what, when, color or shape).

Bathe with a Letter

Materials

Refrigerator magnet letters that float (most do!)

Some plastic refrigerator magnet letters will float and can be used as bath toys. Try using a "W" for water, or a "B" for bath, or even the first letter of your child's name as a bathtime companion.

You can even sing a song about the letter (sing one you know, or make one up). For example (to the tune of "On Top of Old Smokey"): "Here is a B-ee. It sounds like this. 'buh buh buh buh buh.' It stands for Bath."

Variation

Use a number instead. Your child's age is a good one to start with.

Bathtub Science Experiment

Materials

Bathtub

Various items made of wood, plastic or metal

While your toddler bathes, present him with a scientific problem to solve: What will float? Place in the water four or five objects, such as plastic cups, sponges, blocks or spoons, and see which will float. Talk to your child about the various objects: their colors, sizes and what they are used for.

Bathtub Rescue

Materials

Bath toy vehicles (boats, trains, cars)

Introduce your toddler to the idea that 9-1-1 stands for help and
rescue by saving bath toys in distress. Make believe the toy vehicle
(boat, train or car) is "sinking," and encourage her to come to the
rescue with her own toy boat. Say something like, "Help! 9-1-1! Save
the boat! 9-1-1!"

Wash Rocks

Materials
Rocks collected on a nature walk
Soft brush (optional)

On days when you bring rocks home from an outing, use the bathtub
to investigate them. Point out to your toddler how rocks change color
when wet. Submerge them to show how they cannot float on the
water. Let her scrub them with a soft brush.

This is a good opportunity to talk to your child not only about
the rocks, but also about "time." Review the day's activities,
reminding her how you found the rocks during your walk, what else
you saw and did and who you met.

Wash a Dolly

Materials
Doll
Washcloth
Small square plastic toy (optional)
Small plastic bottle filled with water (optional)

Here's a good way to use the bathroom to teach about hygiene and parts of the body. Help your child wash her favorite doll. Use a washcloth and pretend soap (a square plastic toy) and shampoo (a plastic bottle of water). Talk to her about what she's doing.

This activity encourages your toddler to nurture and care for smaller beings—which could be helpful if a younger sibling is in the picture now or comes along later.

Bathtub Catch

Materials
Plastic basket or bucket
Bath toys

Before lifting your toddler out of the tub, help him clean up the bath toys. (He'll learn something, and you won't have rubber duckies and plastic boats to kick around during the next morning's shower.)

Toss the toys into a plastic bucket or basket. The bucket can double as a storage container to hold toys when not in use.

Spruce Up the Bathroom

Materials
Spray bottle filled with water
Paper towels

When you're not concerned with cleaning your toddler, try cleaning the bathroom. Fill a spray bottle with water and let him "wash" the bathroom windows and mirrors, wiping them with a paper towel.

 Do not use window cleaner or newspapers for these activities. Neither product is safe for toddlers.

Variation
If cleaning is not enough fun, try "painting." Fill a bucket with water and give your child a clean brush to paint the shower stall or bathtub.

Toilet Bowl Target Practice

Materials

Ice cube trays
Food coloring
Water

If your son is beginning to think about abandoning diapers, he might enjoy Toilet Bowl Target Practice. There actually are products made for this (claiming to encourage potty learning), but you can do it yourself by making colored ice cubes with food coloring and water. When your toddler has to pee, float an ice cube in the toilet bowl and encourage him to aim for it.

INDEX

About the Author

Nancy Kelly is the owner of Toddler Place, which offers classes for toddlers and their parents. She lives in Stevensville, Maryland. This is her first book.